more than a woman

A Play by Russell Liney

A DISCLAIMER

The factual aspects of the play have been carefully researched from various biographies and autobiographies and moving pictures of Bette Davis's life and career. Liberties have been taken by the author in creating scenes and dialogue that might have taken place, but the words and the actions are of the author's own invention and have been awarded to fictional characters, some of which are based with the greatest respect, on people that existed in real life. All reasonable efforts have been made to contact the copyright holders of the optional and integrated songs and anyone who believes their copyright to be infringed is welcome to contact the author and publisher.

Sylvia,

with love,

Russell

RUSSELL LINEY was born in Leicester in 1957. As a student of the arts, he covered all aspects of design required for working within the advertising industry and became proficient in a variety of art forms: graphic design, illustration, typography, calligraphy, photography, silk screen printing, painting and fine art.

From 1976 he worked in Nottinghamshire and London as a graphic designer and exhibited his personal artwork in London. He later on became a freelance designer and photographer, working for various East Midlands and London-based charities in the production of educational material in the fight against HIV and AIDS.

Since 1991, he has exhibited his photographs and drawings in Leicester and West Yorkshire, and has managed art and photography exhibitions in Leicester.

From 1998 onwards, he began to write scenarios for his own short films and this naturally progressed to larger and more personal written work.
More Than A Woman originated as a screenplay for a short film: The Alley Duse. It caught the imagination of film producer Mark Shivas who thought it worthy of being made, but certain technicalities would prove the film to be too costly to make within the limited budget and the scale of the story too broad to encapsulate within a short running time of 20 minutes.

"Nevertheless, Mark was enthusiastic and encouraged me to develop the piece, either as a play written for radio or an even lengthier version for the stage, both of which could be economically viable productions," Russell says. "His expert advice about the 'less is more' aspect of staging, was to construct the story with an eye fixed firmly on budget limitations. A play for radio requires no sets or costumes. In a play written for the stage, the audience's imagination can be manipulated (but not wholly) by detailed description within the script, and the use of a minimalist set allows each individual in the audience to paint a unique personal visualization onto the blank canvass of the stage.

"With this in mind, I adapted the screenplay into an audio play of 50 minutes duration, also entitled: The Alley Duse. (The audio play has since been revised and renamed An Evening In The Company Of A Fallen Star: which was the original working title.) Although satisfied with the audio script; ultimately, I felt the story was too big to be restricted within the confines of a play for radio. Not wanting to compromise, I extended the story: developing existing characters and adding new: while deconstructing and reconstructing the plot in the creation of the stage play.

"After extended research, numerous rewrites and edits, the finished piece is a play in two acts, preceded by a prologue, titled: *More* Than A Woman."

Cast of Characters

MORE THAN A WOMAN was first performed in an abridged version, by members of Leicester University Theatre at The Queens Hall Theatre, University of Leicester, Leicester, England on 18 June 2015 with the following cast, by order of appearance:

PROLOGUE

Isabella Greenan as RUTHIE DAVIS (1930)

Francesca Leone as BETTE DAVIS (1930)

ACT I ~ THE ALLEY DUSE

Francesca Leone as BETTE DAVIS (1930, 1934 & 1936)

Isabella Greenan as RUTHIE DAVIS (1930)

Sean Thurgood as PERCIVAL HARPER (1930)

Emily Dilworth as BETTE DAVIS (1949)

Bryanie Whittingham-Ball as CHRISTABEL MURGATROYD (1934 & 1936)

Ben Chrome as JACK WARNER (1934 & 1936)

Alex Hatcher as RAMON 'BUD' GABRIELLI (1949)

Isabella Greenan as JOAN CRAWFORD (1946 & 1953)

Daniel Brewer as a PRESS REPORTER

ACT II ~ THE LONELY LIFE

Daniel Brewer as GLENN FORD (1946)

Francesca Leone as BETTE DAVIS (1946 & 1943)

Alex Hatcher as RAMON 'BUD' GABRIELLI (1949 & 1932)

Emily Dilworth as BETTE DAVIS (1949)

Bryanie Whittingham-Ball as MIRIAM HOPKINS (1943)

Sean Thurgood as VINCENT SHERMAN (1943)

Ben Chrome as a CLAPPER BOY (1943)

Daniel Brewer as THOMAS 'THOM' (1932)

Isabella Greenan as MRS O'LEARY (1932)

Isabella Greenan as a TORCH SINGER (1932)

Director & Production Design ~ Russell Liney

Producer & Associate Director ~ Thomas Chiverton

Lighting, Video & Sound Design ~ Miles Orton, Abigail Lane, Luke Stavenuiter & Adam Unwin

Dialogue Coaching & Character Development ~ Susannah Greenan

Stage Manager ~ Amelia Oliver

Wardrobe ~ Thiran Sunder

Characters

BETTE DAVIS [Mature] American Film Actress in 1949, Age 41

BETTE DAVIS [Young to Mature] in 1930, Age 22
1934, Age 26. 1936, Age 28. 1943, Age 35 & 1946, Age 38

RAMON GABRIELLI 'BUD'
American Film Studio Lighting Technician in 1949, Age 38

YOUNG BUD
American Film Studio General Technician in 1932, Age 21

THOMAS 'THOM' [Bud's Partner]
American Film Studio Assistant Choreographer in 1932, Age 19

MIRIAM HOPKINS
American Film Actress in 1943, Age 41

VINCENT SHERMAN
American Film Director in 1943, Age 37

JACK WARNER
American Film Studio Chief in 1934, Age 41 & 1936, Age 43

CHRISTABEL MURGATROYD
Secretary To Jack Warner in 1934, Age 45 & 1936, Age 47

RUTHIE DAVIS Bette's Mother in 1930, Age 45
MR PERCIVAL HARPER Representative of UNIVERSAL PICTURES in 1930
MRS O'LEARY Thom's landlady in 1932
GLENN FORD American Film Actor in 'A STOLEN LIFE' in 1946, Age 30
JOAN CRAWFORD American Film Actress in 1946, Age 42 & 1954, Age 49
BABY JANE HUDSON & BLANCHE HUDSON Characters in 'WHATEVER
HAPPENED TO BABY JANE?' in 1962
CLAPPER BOY on the set of 'OLD ACQUAINTANCE' in 1943
MAKE-UP ASSISTANT on the set of 'OLD ACQUAINTANCE' in 1943
PRESS REPORTER after the death of Joan Crawford in May 1977
[OPTIONAL] TORCH SINGER in 1932
[OPTIONAL] BOO Bette's wire haired fox terrier in 1930

more than a woman

prologue & act one

act two

•

an alternative act one scene one

Authors Notes

The stage directions should be adhered to wherever possible. They are all relevant to the flow and the atmosphere of the drama. The lighting, sound, special effects, songs, entrances and exits are specific and designed to give extra dimensions to the production which is essentially performed on a blank canvass, like a moving picture on the silver screen. A minimalist set is required with no more stage props than are written within the stage directions or than are deemed necessary.

Each scene should flow smoothly and effortlessly from one to the next to give the illusion of continuity as in a moving picture. The play is written and designed to emulate the experience of watching a moving picture.

When the lighting is designed to fade to stage black either during or at the end of a scene, this is meant to resemble a fade-out in a film. Stage black at any point in the play should be brief.

A cast of no less than eight actors is essential. If only eight actors are used in any future production, doubling up will be necessary. In that case, please refer to the original cast list provided and adhere to the doubling as set down therein.

The majority of the songs are optional but nevertheless are essential to the story and so the inclusion of them is preferable wherever possible. *Shuffle Off To Buffalo* and *They're Either Too Young Or Too Old* are not optional and must be included.

Prologue

Saturday 13th December 1930. Stage black.

> [*A single spot lights up on* RUTHIE DAVIS: *she speaks directly to the audience.*]

RUTHIE DAVIS: Ruthie Davis is my name. A 45 year old divorcee and mother of two fine daughters. I'm an independent type and have always been so. Since the day I learned to crawl, I've had the irrepressible desire of an adventurer to know what lies *beyond* the visible horizon.

I was a pretty child but *hated* being a female so I *insisted* on being called Fred. I wore my brother's clothes, played with the boys, and was what is commonly known as a tomboy. I *loved* being one of the boys and they in turn loved me for my unconventional spirit. In their eyes, a girl who didn't mind getting her face mussed and the seat of her pants dirty was swell!

Consequently, in the transition from girl to young woman, I was a late bloomer. But at 19, *flower* I did… and with *style*.

I'd acquired the graceful, gay femininity akin to that of young socialite women in the paintings of Mr John Singer Sargent. So I ditched the Levi pants and baseball mitt, called myself Ruthie and became a woman of fashion… with just a *hint* of tomboy.

> [*Pause.*]

I was artistic and felt the need to express myself creatively so I set my sights on becoming a dancer or an actress. I was a talented creature. Who knows *what* I might have achieved if I *hadn't* married Harlow Morrell Davis. That man, put an end to my grandiose idea of a career. His ideal wife was expected to perform nothing more than was her duty: to serve her husband and raise their children. A suffocating prospect! So I rebelled against what I came to call my enslavement, hoping that at least he might relent a little and meet me half way. But instead, he took up with a compliant mistress and abandoned me along with our two girls, Bette and Barbara.

[RUTHIE *pauses while a second spot lights up on her eldest daughter* BETTE DAVIS.]

We could barely survive on the monthly alimony payments so I became a self-employed portrait photographer and our needs were met.

BETTE DAVIS: [*Impatiently tapping her foot.*] When do we get to the part about *me*, Mother?

RUTHIE: [*Soothingly, to* BETTE.] Soon my chick.

[BETTE *rolls her eyes.*]

[*To the audience.*] This is my daughter Bette. Patience is *not* one of Bette's virtues and she's never one to be left out of the spotlight. *Always* has to be the centre of attention.

[*A pause as* RUTHIE *waits for the spotlight on* BETTE *to fade.*]

Bette was developing a talent for acting! Her pent-up nervous energy was like some elemental force that burned out of her as she performed. I felt she was destined for greatness. When I told Harlow of my intention to enrol Bette into an academy for the dramatic arts, he promptly cut Bette *and* her sister out of his will. It was his way of punishing me for steering Bette *away f*rom marriage and *towards* a career. [*She shouts to the air above.*] Well Harlow, you only made my resolve stronger! [*To the audience.*] Success doesn't get served up to one on a plate. Bette knew she'd have to earn it the hard way, so, woe betide anyone who *dared* to stand in her way.

[*Pause.*]

Her course was set. Before long, Broadway beckoned. Then, suddenly, *Hollywood* came calling at her dressing room door. It all happened, as they say, in a flash.

[*The lights come up fast as the prologue seamlessly runs into act one.*]

Act One

The Alley Duse

Scene One

Saturday 13th December 1930. Midday.
Railway Station Platform. Pasadena, California USA.
Stage actress BETTE DAVIS *and her mother* RUTHIE,
having just arrived, are waiting for an escort to take them to the
UNIVERSAL FILM STUDIO. *Both are smartly but plainly dressed.*
Bette is irritable from the long, cross-country journey and she is pacing
the platform agitatedly. It is a hot, bright sunny day.

BETTE DAVIS: God damn it, Mother! There's nobody here.
   They've forgotten us.

RUTHIE DAVIS: Don't curse Bette dear, and don't worry so. You *know* I
   wired Mr Johnston before we boarded the train in Chicago. He's
   expecting us.

BETTE: Then *where's* the escort he promised?

RUTHIE: Someone is bound to turn up eventually. Why don't you go sit
   in the waiting room? I'll stay here.

BETTE: [*Rubbing her rear.*] We've been sitting for more than *five days* on
   that blasted train Mother, travelling at a snails pace through countless
   miles of snowdrifts with frozen asses. *I* don't mean to sit down again
   for a week.

RUTHIE: Please Bette, 'backsides' or 'rear ends' are quite adequate and acceptable alternatives, you know.

[*They laugh pleasantly.*]

We should thank our lucky stars we are in sunny California. [*She breathes in deeply and exhales loudly.*] What a lovely day! Saturday December 13, 1930 is one we should always remember my love. The start of your career in motion pictures!

BETTE: Isn't it strange? Only twelve days to Christmas and it's like the middle of a New England July.

[*They stand soaking up the sun appreciatively.* MR HARPER, *a representative of* UNIVERSAL PICTURES *makes his entrance via the aisle but stands a way apart from* BETTE *and* RUTHIE, *scrutinising them. He is of medium height with a thin moustache and hair slicked flat, wearing a plain suit and carrying his hat. He is slightly effeminate and fussy – a combination of Eric Blore and Franklin Pangborn.*]

Look Mother! That odd little man over there. Do you suppose…

[MR H *approaches* BETTE *and* RUTHIE, *dabbing at his perspiring forehead with a handkerchief. He stands between the women. He addresses* BETTE *and completely ignores* RUTHIE.]

MR HARPER: Pardon me, but are you by chance a Miss Davis?

BETTE: I am.

MR H: Miss Bette Davis?

BETTE: That's right.

MR H: I'm Mr Percival Harper. [*He takes* BETTE*'s hand and shakes it vigorously.*] On behalf of Mr Carl Laemmle and Mr Laemmle Jr. of Universal Pictures, I'd like to welcome you my dear. I hope your journey was a pleasant one?

BETTE: Barely tolerable, but as you see, I survived it.

[*Still holding her hand,* MR H *looks* BETTE *up and down from head to toe.*]

MR H: Well… my dear… you're not what I was expecting. No, not one bit. I'd imagined you to be quite… different.

BETTE: [*Quite taken aback, rapidly withdrawing her hand.*] *How* different, *Mr* Harper?

MR H: You don't look like any actress *I've* met, my dear.

BETTE: [*Sharply, due to his directness.*] Is that so? Just what kind of person *did* you expect? A pouting, peroxide blonde perhaps?

MR H: You jest my dear, but at the very *least,* you should own a fur coat and wear *expensive* perfume. The very *best*. Mitsouko! Shalimar! Not… [*He sniffs the air, disapprovingly.*] Lily of the Valley.

BETTE: A fur coat for the journey here *would* have been both welcome and practical, but in this heat. Are you kidding, Mr Harper?

MR H: My dear young lady, I'm serious. From today, your public image is of paramount importance. In a crowd of *ordinary* people, you have to stand out larger than life, and cultivate a personal style all your own to set you apart from your peers. Then there's Mr *Laemmle* to please. *His* priority will be to see how your gams rate.

BETTE: My what?

MR H: Your legs! He appreciates a good shapely leg on a well-dressed woman.

BETTE: That may be, but what have my *legs* got to do with acting?

MR H: [*Droll and bitchy.*] My dear… it's *clear* you're new to Hollywood. [*He circles* BETTE *once, looking her over, speaking at the same time.*] Your attire *does* hint at a vague artistic… *some*thing, but *you* will have to be completely made over.
[*He scratches his head in bewilderment.*] Er… where was I?

BETTE: You were expressing how plain I look.

MR H: Now please, my dear, I don't mean to imply *anything* of the kind. Good gracious no. But, you have to admit, you're no bird of paradise, more like a little brown wren *I'd* say. Never mind, we'll take care of *that*. Now, if you will allow me, I have a car waiting to take you to the Hollywood Plaza Hotel and, from there, to meet Mr Laemmle.

[*He turns, dismounts the stairs and waits halfway down the aisle.* BETTE *and* RUTHIE *laugh in disbelief at his complete lack of subtlety.*]

BETTE: [*To* RUTHIE.] Welcome to California! Hold my arm, Mother. I feel the insuperable urge to slap that man. Will *all* studio executives be so damned rude I wonder?

RUTHIE: I think our Mr Harper is more likely to be a mere lackey.
Mr Laemmle's pumped up errand boy.

BETTE: [*Calls out.*] Oh, Mr Harper!

[MR H *returns to front centre stage.*]

You *may* not have noticed this lady patiently waiting. It is my mother.
She is going to accompany me when I meet with Mr Laemmle.

[MR H, *flustered, acknowledges* RUTHIE.]

MR H: I beg your pardon my dear lady. [*He takes* RUTHIE's *hand and
bends to kiss it but thinks twice and drops it due to her angry
expression.*] Pleased to… er… make your acquaintance I'm sure.
[*To* BETTE.] Dear Miss Davis… or might I call you Bette?

BETTE: Bette… *if* you must.

MR H: Mr Laemmle will *insist* on seeing you alone Bette. He doesn't
approve of stage mothers tagging along.

RUTHIE: *Really?* Well I'm hardly one of *those* Mr Harper. You should get
to know me a little better before making an assumption of *that* kind.

MR H: I can tell you now, it's extremely unlikely that a mother of *any* kind
will get her foot in the door of Mr Laemmle's office.

BETTE: Then, Mr Harper, this will be one of those rare occasions where
one *does*. Where I go, Mother goes, or I don't go at all. Why, she's
given up almost everything she owns to finance this trip and if it
weren't for her complete faith in my talent, I'd not be here today.

[BETTE *slips an arm around* RUTHIE's *waist. Looking directly at* RUTHIE, *she speaks with sincere affection.*]

Ruthie, you are nothing short of being a saint! [*Turning her head to address* MR H.] And… when I'm a star, I'll see she lives in a style that befits a star's mother.

MR H: My oh my, you're an outspoken young lady aren't you my dear? Film Star indeed! You *are* in a hurry. Well nobody could say you're not determined. [*To* RUTHIE, *flustered.*] Ruth… er… *Mrs* Davis. I hope that you can persuade Bette to hold her fire when she meets Mr Laemmle. Her future at Universal might depend on it.

RUTHIE: I am responsible for nurturing Bette's independent spirit, Mr Harper. She doesn't require my advice when it comes to dealing with studio heads or making her own career decisions. Do you, love?

BETTE: Certainly not!

RUTHIE: Even if she *does* hang herself in the process. [*She pauses briefly.*] But a word of warning. If you ever light Bette's fuse, stand as far away as possible as quickly as you can. It's a very short one.

MR H: [*Ruffled and resigned.*] Very well madam, after this little demonstration I think I shall take that as good advice. We had better be getting along.

[MR H *leaves the stage via the stairs and begins a slow exit via the aisle.*]

BETTE: Don't be fooled, Mother. I'm nervous *and* apprehensive on the inside.

RUTHIE: Our Mr Harper doesn't know that, does he? You fooled *him*.
Be tough with these guys Bette. Have 'em by the balls from the word
go. It's a man's world my love, so you're going to have to be *more*
than a woman if you mean to rise in it. Show them you mean
business – they'll take you seriously.

BETTE: If you weren't here, Mother, I'd be on the next train back home.

RUTHIE: I'll stick around for as long as you need me. For the duration if
you like.

[MR H *calls to them from the aisle.*]

MR H: Well ladies, have you changed your minds?

[BETTE *and* RUTHIE *exchange amused glances.*]

BETTE: Lead on Mr Harper.

[BETTE *links her arm in* RUTHIE'*s. They march off stage via the
steps and exit, following* MR H *via the aisle.*]

RUTHIE: Let battle commence!

Scene Two

*Evening. A deserted street on an exterior film set at the Warner Brothers
Studio, Hollywood in 1949. From the aisle, furthest from the stage, slurred
singing is heard, slightly out of* tune. BETTE DAVIS, *age 41, makes an
aisle entrance holding a half-empty glass of whisky in one hand and a
large purse with handles in the other, which visibly contains two bottles of
whisky, one already opened, and an Oscar statuette.*

The song she is engaged in is, 'Shuffle Off To Buffalo'. She walks regally but drunkenly. She has shoulder-length waved hair. She is wearing a stunningly expensive knee-length dress with elbow-length sleeves, gathered at the waist by a thick belt, a wispy silk scarf tied at the side of the neck, a large diamond brooch pinned above her left breast, seamed stockings and luxurious high-heeled shoes. She continues singing as she makes her way along the aisle in order to mount the stairs to the stage.

[*Now on stage, she ceases singing abruptly. A brief pause.*]

BETTE DAVIS: [*Slurring.*] Well! Oscar… what have we here? A billboard poster for my latest creative endeavour, or should I say… turkey! [*She quotes loudly.*] "Coming soon! Warner Brothers Pictures presents 'Beyond The Forest' starring Bette Davis. *Nobody's* as good as *Bette* when she's bad!" The studio advertising department really busted their brains thinking up *that* phrase. Bad? Awful! Ridiculous! Worse even! Well, if the caption fits, I guess I'll have to wear it. That God damn son-of-a-bitch Jack Warner! 17 years of working out my guts to become the studio's biggest asset and *this* is how he finally repays me.
I said… "What're you trying to prove by casting me as Rosa? I'm *40*, Jack. Who's going to believe I'm a young woman of *25*?" [*She groans in despair.*] Rosa Moline! He should've asked Mayer to loan out Lana Turner or just given it to Virginia Mayo. Either one would've been a better choice. "*And… I'm* just not the *type* for that part", I told him! Begged him to reconsider… the bastard wouldn't listen to reason. Did he *ever* listen?

[*Lights up fast on the rear stage: preferably raised. The action flows quickly and smoothly into scene three.*]

Scene Three

1934. Rear stage: preferably raised. JACK WARNER's *office and reception area. Lights up fast.* JACK WARNER *is seated at his desk. He is wearing a pin-stripe suit, shirt and tie. He has a pencil-line moustache. His secretary,* CHRISTABEL MURGATROYD *enters his office. She is wearing a conservative two-piece suit, blouse, spectacles, and medium-heeled laced shoes. Her hairstyle is a tight 'Marcel' wave.*

CHRISTABEL MURGATROYD: Excuse me Mr Warner.

JACK WARNER: Yes, what is it, Miss Murgatroyd?

MISS M: I've just had word from security that Miss Davis is on her way up to see you.

WARNER: [*Rising from his seat.*] *What?* Jesus! Didn't I tell them not to let her into the building at *any* price?

MISS M: Well she got past them and she's in the elevator.

WARNER: Dear God… the woman's unstoppable. She's absolutely determined I loan her out to R K O to play a common *waitress.* Where's the glamour in *that*?

MISS M: *Glamour*? Bette's not cut out for glamour and she'd be the first to admit it. What she needs is a challenge. I've read Mr Maugham's book, sir. It will make a great picture and I think Bette's *perfect* for the part.

WARNER: Oh you do? Since when did I give you authority over casting, Murgatroyd?

MISS M: It's an honest opinion, sir.

WARNER: Well here's *mine*. Bette has the crazy notion it will make her a star but I know better. It'll destroy her!

MISS M: Whatever you say, sir, but she'll be here shortly and if security couldn't stop her, how do you expect *me* to?

WARNER: Use your imagination! Do anything you can to keep her away from me. I can't take another of her hysterical tirades.

MISS M: I could try wrestling her to the floor. *That* might subdue her.

WARNER: This is no time to get smart with me, Murgatroyd. How many more times must I stress that *on no account* are you to let that cunt into my office?

[*A long silence.* MISS M *stares contemptuously at* WARNER.]

Miss Murgatroyd… do you hear me?

MISS M: [*A rebellious undertone.*] Yes *sir!* I hear you. I'll do my very best.

[MISS M *turns on her heel and exits* WARNER's *office.*
BETTE DAVIS, *age 26, enters the reception area, expensively attired. She's in a fury, eyes popping out of her head, ready for a showdown with* WARNER.]

[*Genuinely sincere but business-like.*] Ah! Good afternoon, Miss Davis. It's so *very* nice to see you again. My… that's a lovely ensemble your wearing. The style suits you so well.

BETTE: [*Impatiently pacing the stage, she nods in response.*] Thanks, Murgatroyd.

MISS M: And how is your dear mother?

BETTE: Fitter than a Strad-i-varius. Given the chance, she'd be here for a showdown with Mr Warner on my behalf. They don't make 'em like Ruthie any more.

MISS M: Oh but they *do*, Miss Davis. You are very much like your Mother! Please pass on my *very* best wishes to the admirable lady.

BETTE: Certainly I will Murgatroyd. *Now*, if you don't mind, can we dispense with the pleasantries and move on? [*Continues drily.*] I am wearing the shine off the floor. [*Short pause.*] Mr Warner is currently engaged I take it?

MISS M: On the contrary, Mr Warner's aware you're here, Miss Davis. He said he'd be pleased to see you and you're to go right on in. [*Short pause.*] Oh… and Miss Davis! In future, would you mind if we dropped the formalities? I *think* we know each other well enough. I'd like it *very* much if you'd call me Christa and I hope you won't mind if I call you Bette?

BETTE: [*Surprised but kindly.*] Why no… not at all, Christa. [*With her knuckles on her hips,* BETTE *slow marches across reception and into* WARNERS*'s office slamming the door behind her. The lights begin to go down to stage black.*] Trying to give me the brush-off again huh? You… unspeakable *coward*. You snake!

WARNER: [*Bellowing from darkness.*] Murgatroyd!

Scene Four

1949. A continuation of scene two. Lights up fast.

BETTE: Oh, the countless times I have fought with that man. *Exhausting!* C'mon Oscar… let's you and me have another drink.

[*She tops up her glass and begins to sing a verse from a different song: 'They're Either Too Young Or Too Old'.*]

[*At the conclusion of the verse she burps loudly, and laughs raucously.*] Christ! I'm drunk and my feet *hurt*. Think I need to sit down. Not very lady-like, but this will have to do.

[*She sits on a wide stoop, that has decorative iron-work bannisters on either side, rising up to a doorway. She sets down the whisky glass and purse.*]

Now if only I could kick off these *damn new shoes*. [*Toe to heel, she tries to force off a shoe. She fails, groans and then sighs.*] No, they're too tight.

[RAMON GABRIELLI *otherwise known as* BUD *or* BUDDY *has been observing* BETTE. *He is standing partly in shadow in the aisle, furthest from the stage.* BUD *is tall and muscular, a manly Robert Mitchum/Robert Ryan type. He has a slick hairstyle and is clean-shaven. He is wearing a white casual shirt with breast pockets, worn open at the neck with the sleeves rolled up to his elbows, loose casual pants and smart, laced shoes.*]

BUD: Hey! Miss Davis.

BETTE: Huh?

BUD: Y' need some help?

BETTE: Do I *look* like I need help?

> [BUD *makes his way quickly along the aisle and ascends the stairs to the stage.*]

BUD: Frankly, yes. Saw you sitting there and thought you must've had a fall.

BETTE: [*More to herself than to* BUD.] No. My *star* has fallen, but *I'm* okay, all things considered.

> [BUD *is on stage at this point, keeping a respectful distance.*]

BUD: What're you doing out here on the lot all by yourself, Miss Davis?

BETTE: I am not by myself. I have Oscar here for company. [*She holds up the statuette proudly.*] Don't I, Oscar?

BUD: Err… Pardon my saying so, Miss Davis, but you don't look so good.

BETTE: Don't feel too good either. I'm on a toot! [*She brandishes the glass.*] Thanks to my Scottish friend here, I'm well an' truly soused! [*Commanding.*] Come over *here*, so I can take a better look at you. I can't get up! [BUD *does as he is told.*] Well! Buddy Gabrielli! Forgive me and my big mouth. These shoes are killing my feet! I've tried to remove them but they're stuck tight. Take them off for me, will you Bud? If I lean forward any further I'm likely to roll off the side-walk and into the gutter.

BUD: [*Amused.*] Why sure.

[*He removes her shoes.*]

BETTE: Ah *what* a relief!

BUD: Miss Davis, it's your last day at Warner's. Me and the crew, we've been looking for you *all over* the lot. We were beginning to think you must've skipped the joint early. You deserve a proper send-off. Don't you want a farewell party?

BETTE: I told *Mr Warner* I didn't want any fuss.

BUD: What about your friends?

BETTE: My friends would rather be home than with me when I'm like *this*.

BUD: Your colleagues then. Where the hell *is* everyone?

BETTE: All safely tucked up in bed where they belong I guess! Oh, I've no doubt that there are a God damn few who *will* celebrate tonight… those who are glad to see me go. I was just happy to be on my own. But since you're here Bud, [*She pats the step she is sitting on.*] come and sit by me. That's an invitation, not an order. [BUD *hesitates.*] *C'mon…* I won't bite. Here! Take a drink of whisky with me. Let's share some of the past times we've had here at the studio.

BUD: Okay, Miss Davis, if you insist. [BETTE *hands him the open bottle.* BUD *sits and takes a long gulp.*] Cigarette, Miss Davis?

BETTE: Best words in the English language. I smoked my last a half hour ago. I could *kill* for one!

18

[BUD *takes a pack of cigarettes and matches from his shirt breast pocket. He lights two simultaneously, and then offers one to* BETTE.]

BUD: Here you are Miss Davis.

[*They draw on their cigarettes simultaneously.*]

BETTE: Thank you Bud and, please, call me Bette. [*A pause while she smiles knowingly.*] What a charming gesture. Lighting them both and then offering one to me, just as Paul Henreid did in 'Now Voyager'. What a romantic moment that was and what a great film. But of course… you worked on that one, didn't you?

BUD: Sure did! Moonlighting courtesy of Bud Gabrielli!

BETTE: Look at that indigo and orange sky, Bud. Isn't it amazing? Puts Technicolor in the shade. Have you ever in your life seen so violent a sunset? All the turmoil, hard work, and battles I fought here seem to be summed up in that sky. There's no moon yet… a scattering of stars though… *they'll* do! [*She takes a brief thoughtful pause.*] I was remembering the time, some years ago, I made a picture called 'Kid Galahad'. In the final scene, I walked along a deserted city street, much like this one, and disappeared into the night and towards an uncertain future. Now, here I am doing it again, but this time for real! The Alley Duse!

BUD: The Alley Duse? I've heard that before. What is it?

BETTE: A film critic once called me that. To be compared to the great stage actress Eleonora Duse was the *biggest* compliment I could have wished for back then.

BUD: Then I consider it an honour to be the only person celebrating here tonight with the great *screen* actress, Bette Davis. [*He raises the bottle in the air.*] A toast! To the Queen of Warner Brothers!

BETTE: The queen? Not for some time. No… the *new* Queen of Warner Brothers will be toasting my departure tonight. That's something I *am* certain of.

BUD: Y' mean Crawford?

BETTE: Well I had hoped she'd remain nameless, but yes. *Saint Joan.*

[*Lights down fast to stage black. Flashback to 1946. A single spotlight on* JOAN CRAWFORD, *age 42. She is standing centre of the rear raised stage and is wearing a full-length satin bed-robe with a fur trim collar and satin slippers.*]

JOAN CRAWFORD: Thank you all, for gathering here outside my home tonight to share my success. You don't know how much it means to me to have your love and support. So I dedicate this award to you *all*. My devoted fans. Bless you! I love you. Bless you all! And now, my beloved children and I, wish you *goodnight*. [*Spotlight out.*]

BETTE: [*Spoken from darkness with sarcasm.*] Nice speech, Joan. *Bonne nuit!* [*Lights up fast.*] *Beloved* children. That's rich! Who's she trying to kid? She thinks more of her beloved *fans* than she does her children. She adopted those kids purely for the publicity, you know. When her career at MGM was on the skids, she needed a new angle to keep her fans from straying, so she whisked up an instant brood and, 'hey presto', Joan became 'Mommie Dearest'! She's been playing *un*happy families ever since. [*Mock confidentiality.*] There's a rumour that she beat her daughter black and blue with a God damn coat hanger. And Jack Warner thinks she's a *saint!* So she won him an Oscar for playing Mildred Pierce. [*Instantly, she's on her feet,* *forcefully expelling smoke*.] Well big deal! *I* won him *two!* I've had enough of that cheap bastard and the crap he's thrown at me through the years and I'm not playing second fiddle to that *fucking bitch* Joan. [*Lights down fast to stage black, leaving just a spotlight on* BETTE, *speaking directly to the audience, à la* REGINA GIDDENS *in 'The Little Foxes'.*] Ah hope she dies! Ah hope she dies soon. Ah'll be waiting for her to die! [*Lights up fast.* BETTE *as herself.*] You can't have two queen bees in the same hive you know. One will either drive the other out… or kill her.

[JOAN CRAWFORD, *age 49, has entered, standing centre of the rear raised stage as* VIENNA, *a character she will play in the 1953 film 'Johnny Guitar'.* JOAN *is wearing the masculine cowboy outfit she will wear in the film. She draws a pistol from her holster and aims at* BETTE.]

Look at her. Just *who* does she think she is? Standing up there, like she's *somebody*. Looking down on *us* like we're nobody.

VIENNA (JOAN): Down there I sell whisky and deal cards. Up here, all you can buy is a bullet in the head. Now which do you want?

BETTE: [*To the audience*.] Well, if that's the choice, I'll have a whisky. On second thought, better make that a double!

[VIENNA (JOAN) *exits,* BUD *stands, and a* PRESS REPORTER *enters stage right as* BETTE *pours herself a double.*]

[*To* BUD.] When Joan dies and the gentlemen of the press ask me…

PRESS REPORTER: "Miss Davis! In spite of the ongoing rivalry between yourself and Miss Crawford, now that she's dead, is there *one* good thing you can say about her?"

BETTE: [*To* BUD.] I shall say… [*To the* PRESS REPORTER.] "Well she's *dead* isn't she? So, *good!*"

[BETTE *and* BUD *fall about laughing. The* PRESS REPORTER *exits.*]

BUD: Who knows… someday you and Crawford might get to star in the same picture.

BETTE: *What?* Now *there's* a twisted idea! One day, you mean, when we've both laid to rest our professional or should I say, *petty,* rivalries?

BUD: Somebody ought to suggest it to Mr Warner.

BETTE: Over my dead! I can see us now. Two washed-up old broads playing the two ugly sisters. *What* a queer pantomime *that* would be. Hollywood royalty, la *Joanie* and box office poison, yours truly.

Optional: [*Lights down fast to stage black. A piano introduction is heard from darkness. A large spot lights up stage left on* JOAN CRAWFORD, *age 57, as* BLANCHE HUDSON. BLANCHE *is sitting at a piano and the piano hides the fact that she is in a wheelchair.* BLANCHE *plays 'I've Written A Letter To Daddy' from 'Whatever Happened To Baby Jane?', a film that* JOAN *and* BETTE *will make together in 1962. A baby-spot lights up on* BETTE DAVIS, *age 54, as* BABY JANE HUDSON. BABY JANE *dances and sings the verse. Off-stage, a* BARBER SHOP QUARTET *repeat the verse during which,* BABY JANE *and* BLANCHE, *(followed by the large spot) dance a comical 'wheelchair waltz'.* BABY JANE, *returns* BLANCHE *to the piano in time for* BLANCHE *to resume playing the concluding line of the song while* BABY JANE *returns to the baby spot to sing and dance the concluding line of the song.*

Both spots on BABY JANE *and* BLANCHE *fade to stage black. Lights up fast.*] Optional: concludes.

BETTE: No, *this* old cow is moving on to graze in pastures new. [*Pause.*] You know what the bitter truth is Bud? The kind of woman's pictures I made are finished, at least for a while anyway. They've served their purpose. When our men went to war, women found romantic fantasy in my films. Now the war's over, the men have returned and so has romantic reality. I'm getting older. I have to face the fact that I can no longer get away with playing the younger romantic parts. Now *Joan*, with all her airs and graces is too precious to *ever* admit she's growing older. In her imagination she's *still* a spring chicken, so she dresses accordingly. Right down to those *awful* 'chase me, fuck me' shoes. She looks like an ageing hooker who's out for some kicks. If she lives to be a *hundred*, she'll still be wearing those damn shoes. When you feel like a 20-year-old on the inside, but appear 40 on the outside, it's then you realise that ageing is a fucking bitch of an ugly joke!

Optional: [*The lights begin to slowly fade down to stage black.* BETTE *moves to front centre stage where she is lit, directly from above by a small spot.* BETTE *sings 'Growing Older, Feeling Younger', to the audience.*] Optional: concludes.

BUD: So, what's the answer?

BETTE: I have to adapt to survive and make way for a younger generation of actresses [*With sarcasm.*] by *gracefully* accepting, shall we say, the more *mature* roles. Well I'm a game gal! I don't ever want to be a redundant has-been. [*Seriously.*] To keep on working is the thing. It's my raison d'etre. That… and my child. [*Pause.*] In spite of everything though, I *will* miss this place. It's been my *home* for 17 years.

BUD: And I'm sure as Hell going to miss you. Working with you has been a real pleasure, Miss Davis.

BETTE: Damn it, I asked you to call me *Bette!*

BUD: If you insist… *Bette*. Some of the best times I can recall were when I was working on your pictures. Remember how we used to applaud you at the end of those sensational takes? We'd go wild! And y' know why? You always had time for *us*. Appreciated all our hard work. Made us feel we weren't just a means to an end. When Crawford gives out the praise, it seems false somehow, insincere. She's only got time for herself.

BETTE: That's the truth! I've always respected a good crew and you are a *genius* when it comes to lighting a scene Bud, though no amount of good lighting could hide the fact that I'm too old to be playing the likes of Rosa Moline. Rosa is supposed to be sex on legs with the face of a Jennifer Jones or a Rita Hayworth. Not… this! No mature actress in her right mind would *consider* playing that part. It took a lot of coaxing by Mr Warner to get *me* to do it. I was unconvinced, but when a woman gets to a certain age Bud, it's hard to accept that her youth and femininity are disappearing fast. 'There's a slim chance,' I thought, trying to kid myself, 'that I could pull this off.' [*Humorously.*] Now, *I'm* no glamour-puss. I've never had *that* kind of allure but I decided to give it all I'd got. And my all, more often than not, is what the French call de tro*p*. [*She deliberately sounds the P in trop.*] *My* Rosa Moline struts her stuff like a third-rate female impersonator! Boy, what a travesty. [*They laugh together raucously, nearly to crying.*] I've hit rock bottom, Bud. *That's* a God damn fact!

BUD: Maybe you should ask for the moon again, Bette. One more chance to prove you've still got what it takes. A *great* part, one that'll put you right back at the top, where you belong. You wan' another cigarette?

BETTE: Why not? [*He lights two simultaneously and offers her one.*] Back at the top! [*Thoughtful pause.*] Fifteen years ago, Bud, I was just another unknown actress with great aspirations, starting at the bottom. I made four or five pictures a year. A few were of average merit but most were crappy as hell. 'Parachute Jumper' springs to mind as one of the worst ever. They weren't remotely good parts either, mainly hard-boiled sisterly types, but the occasional good scene got me noticed. I needed a big break. I was screaming inside with frustration for a demanding role. Then I heard that R K O were looking for an actress to play Mildred in 'Of Human Bondage'. [*Pause.*] Mildred was such a cold, unsympathetic, common bitch. No established actress would chance playing her. I was the right age. I had nothing to lose. I *knew* Mildred would be the making of me. John Cromwell, the director, wanted me to play her, but Jack Warner refused to loan me out. He told me I'd be kissing goodbye to my career in pictures. I knew better! So, every day for six months, I hounded him and I yelled at him until he gave in. [*Pause, followed by a long sigh from* BETTE.] I have *never* worked harder than I did in preparing to play Mildred. It paid off. That performance really got me noticed. But in spite of the critical acclaim, Warner deliberately continued to put me in mediocre pictures. Then out of the blue, *success!*
I played Joyce Heath, a down-and-out alcoholic actress in 'Dangerous' and won the Oscar for Best Actress. [BETTE *continues, speaking to* 'OSCAR', *holding the statuette aloft.*] Didn't I, Oscar? Winning *you* should have secured me the best scripts. You brought in some great publicity for Jack *shit-head*. [*To* BUD.] But for all of that, the bastard *still* wouldn't acknowledge my potential or what an asset I was to the studio. Me winning the Oscar seemed to have the opposite effect and he set about to spite me at every turn. I truly believe that

man wanted to destroy my career. But I was having *none of it*. One way or another, I was determined that Warner was going to meet his match! [*The action flows quickly and smoothly into scene five.*]

Scene Five

1936. Rear stage: preferably raised. JACK WARNER's *office and reception area.* MISS M *is speaking to* WARNER *in his office.* WARNER *is seated at his desk.*

MISS M: [*Brightly.*] Oh Mr Warner! Miss Davis is on her way up to see you. [*She sits on* WARNER's *desk and crosses her legs.*] I thought I'd warn you seeing as she *doesn't* have an appointment.

WARNER: When has she *ever* seen me by appointment? Is there *any* point in asking you to keep her out, Murgatroyd?

MISS M: Well if you were to ask me politely, sir, I'd try. But you *know* from experience she'll get past me anyhow.

WARNER: What did security say *exactly?*

MISS M: That she's crimson with fury and fighting mad!

WARNER: That's nothing new. You know, I think I like Bette *more* when she's in a fighting mood, Murgatroyd! I've grown to enjoy our regular spats. She'll be all riled-up over that new script I sent her. 'God's Country and the Woman'. Can you see Bette as a female lumberjack, Murgatroyd?

MISS M: I can imagine her taking a swing at *you* with an axe, sir.

[BETTE DAVIS, *Age 28, enters* MISS M's *reception area and slams the door loudly behind her. She is carrying a film script and her Academy Award statuette.*]

That's her now. I'll know she's cut you down to size, *Mr Warner,* when she cries, 'Timmmberrrr'!

WARNER: Get *out,* Murgatroyd!

[MISS M *turns on her heel and leaves* WARNER's *office.*]

MISS M: Ah, Bette. Ready for action I see. [*She gestures with her thumb for* BETTE *to enter* WARNER's *office.*] Enter with my blessing sister. Remember, go straight for his jugular.

[BETTE *marches through into* WARNER's *office.*]

BETTE: You've got *some* nerve. I won the Academy Award and what did I get in return for my efforts? Three *crummy* pictures in a row, that's what! *Now* you expect me to accept *this* crap! What the *hell* are you trying to do to me?

WARNER: You told me you liked 'The Petrified Forest'.

BETTE: What I *said* was "I'd jump at the chance to play opposite Leslie Howard again." The so-called *film* was dismal and my role mediocre to say the least. And after that, not one, but *two* shitty pictures. 'The Golden Arrow' was second-rate crap. 'Satan Met a Lady', third-rate crap. Well, I'm a *first-rate* actress and I *demand* a first-rate script. [*She brandishes the script.*] Not… *this!* [*She slams the script down onto* WARNER's *desk, then continues sarcastically.*] 'God's Country and the Woman'. It's absolute tripe and I won't do it!

WARNER: Come now Bette, calm down. You'll have George Brent as your co-star and it'll be in colour.

BETTE: Do you *really* believe that throwing in some colour will make it a good film? The script stinks. I'm building up a good reputation as a serious actress, the most viable commodity the God damn studio has. [*She brandishes her Academy Award.*] I was awarded *this!* You're a businessman for Christ's sake. Why aren't you capitalising on it? [*She pauses, then continues more calmly.*] Mr Warner... please. You and I *both* have the opportunity of producing some great pictures, but you are constantly holding me back on purpose. It is *intolerable!* Well I'm not going to make this one, and that is final. A *lumberjack!* Next, you'll be asking me to start shaving.

WARNER: You mean you don't already? [*He makes a calming gesture for* BETTE *to sit down.*] Listen, Bette. 'God's Country' has...

BETTE: Don't forget 'The Woman'.

WARNER: 'God's Country *and the Woman'* has already gone into pre-production. If you'll be reasonable and do this picture, I *promise* you a great role when you finish. I've just optioned a wonderful novel that isn't out yet. It's called 'Gone with the Wind' and Bette... you were *born* to play the heroine.

BETTE: Yeah? I'll bet it's a pip! Good*bye!*

[BETTE *turns on her heel and marches out of* WARNER*'s office.*]

WARNER: Bette! Come *back,* you hear me? *Murgatroyd!*

[BETTE *and* MISS M *cross paths.* BETTE *exits the reception as* MISS M *enters* WARNER*'s office.* WARNER *is on his feet.*]

WARNER: 'Goodbye!' What's she mean by *that?* She's under contract. *Nobody* walks out on a contract with Jack Warner.

MISS M: She just did, sir.

WARNER: Then she'd better return and quick damn it! If not I'll have her arrested and *brought* back. Call my lawyer, Murgatroyd! [MISS M *just stands there, amused, with her arms folded while* WARNER *rants to himself and paces.*] So Bette's running the studio now is she? Demanding this, demanding that. [*To* MISS M.] *I'm* the one in charge around here and what I say *goes!* Who the *hell* does the self-important hysterical cunt think she is anyhow?

MISS M: Mr Warner! The C U N T as you have often referred to her is *the most talented* and *ambitious* young lady it has been your privilege to employ. I may only be your humble secretary, sir, and my opinion probably doesn't count for much, but here it is nevertheless. Treat her fairly and with the *respect* she is due. Bette is no ordinary actress and she will prove you wrong, sir. I believe that some day, she will be hailed as one of our great American actresses, perhaps even the greatest. [*She pauses for breath.*] Oh, she'll be back alright. But it will be on *her* terms, because Mr Warner she *is* what you won't admit she is.

WARNER: [*Wearily.*] And just what is *that*, Miss Murgatroyd?

MISS M: She's more than a match for you… and she's *more* than a woman.

[WARNER *slowly sits at his desk.*]

WARNER: [*Through clenched teeth.*] Get… my… lawyer. [*Heaving. Close to tears from the anger of defeat.*] I… want… Bette… *back.*

MISS M: [*Ignoring* WARNER *she begins to leave his* office.] Touching. He can't live with her and he can't live without her.

WARNER: Cut out the wise-ass remarks Murgatroyd! My lawyer… call him *now!*

MISS M: [*She turns to face him from a distance and salutes.*] Yes, *sir!* Right away, *sir!* And I'll reserve a ringside seat for myself. I want to be right up close when the battle of the heavyweights final takes place.

[WARNER *is amused by her comment and chuckles. The tension relaxes.*]

WARNER: Murgatroyd… remind me to fire you.

MISS M: [*The lights slowly fade to black as* MISS M *exits* WARNER*'s office, singing provocatively.*] "For she's a jolly good fellow, for she's a jolly good fellow, for she's a jolly good fell-ow… that, nobody can deny."

Scene Six

1949. A continuation of scene four. Lights up fast.

BETTE: And so, finally, I walked!

BUD: Walking out on Jack Warner was a hell of a risky thing to do. Risky *and* brave.

BETTE: It sure was a gamble. But Bette Davis plays to *win!*

I couldn't stand being forced to perform by the lash of Warner's whip in this *circus* any longer. My salvation, or so I thought, came with the offer of making a film in England. Meanwhile Warner sent his lawyer in hot pursuit and I was taken to the English courts for breaking my contract. The judge told me, and I quote, "You are like a naughty child who has ungratefully turned on the family that has raised her." Okay! So this 'naughty child' lost the fight but, on returning to Hollywood, in a curious way I found I'd *won!*

At last, Warner had conceded and given up the fight. He'd been impressed by my 'performance' in standing up to him. He realised he had a star in the making and he really began to take me seriously. The script I came home to was 'Marked Woman'. It was a great part and a good story that tackled the serious side of prostitution and gambling. I played a clip joint 'hostess' who was brave enough to take on the mob… and *win*.

[*Lights fade to stage black.*]

End of Act One.

Act Two
The Lonely Life

Scene Seven

A reconstructed scene from the 1946 film, 'A Stolen Life'.
The lantern house at the top of the Dragon-head Lighthouse.
BETTE DAVIS, *age 38, as* KATE, *is exploring the lighthouse.*
She encounters GLENN FORD, *age 30, playing the role of* BILL. *He is laying down, adjusting a part of the lantern bearings. The light is turning, fog drifts all over the stage and a fog horn sounds eerily throughout the scene where indicated.* KATE *enters via the aisle, makes her way to the stage, mounts the steps onto the stage and encounters* BILL *by the end of Fog Horn 2.*

[*Fog Horn 1.*]

[*Long pause.*]

[*Fog Horn 2.*]

GLENN FORD as BILL: Found something to occupy your time?

BETTE DAVIS as KATE: Oh… just taking a look around.

BILL: As you're here, you might hand me the wrench. It's over there.

KATE: I'm glad I didn't try to sail back to the island in this fog.

BILL: You were right to stay. The fog… does it frighten you?

KATE: Only a little.

[*Fog Horn 3.*]

It makes me feel so very lonely. I don't mind being by my*self* but I don't like to feel lonely.

BILL: Loneliness can be a terrible thing.

[*She nods in agreement.*]

I don't mind being alone either. In fact, I took this job of lighthouse keeper to get away from people.

KATE: I can understand that.

[*Fog Horn 4.*]

BILL: You wouldn't be afraid of that fog if you went right out into it. Come on I'll show you.

[*He leads her outside the lantern house onto the circular platform.*]

[*Fog Horn 5.*]

KATE: It's like the end of the world.

BILL: The world *might* end like this.

KATE: I don't think I'd be frightened if it did.

BILL: Or lonely?

[*Fog Horn 6.*]

KATE: Not if *you* were with me. [*Pause.*] If the world *should* end like this, people would have the time to say all the things they'd always wanted to. Then they'd find the courage to say them. [*Pause.*] *Honest* things.

BILL: Such as?

[*Fog Horn 7.*]

KATE: Such as telling you I didn't particularly want to come out here just to paint your portrait.

BILL: Then why did you come; why go to all that trouble?

KATE: 'Cause I wanted to see you again Bill. And perhaps get to know you better.

[*Fog Horn 8.*]

KATE: Lonely people have to search very hard to find friends. It's difficult for them to… to find…

BILL: … other lonely people.

[*Fog Horn 9.*]

[*Pause.*] The fog's lifting.

KATE: [*Softly as the lights fade to stage black.*] It wasn't the end of the world, after all.

34

Scene Eight

1949. A continuation of act one: scene six. Lights up fast.

BUD: So Bette Davis triumphed over Jack Warner!

BETTE: Yeah! And after that, all the good scripts were offered to me.

BUD: You deserved them after all.

BETTE: Sure I did! 'Jezebel', 'The Old Maid', 'Dark Victory', 'The Little Foxes'... and so on. Big budget productions earning big box office returns. Warner's investment was paying out.

BUD: And *you* kept on delivering the goods.

BETTE: Boy didn't I just! I'd fought for those parts, so I had to keep on proving to both myself *and* him that I was worthy of them by giving *more* than my best. Nothing less would do for me. I made four major pictures through 1941 and the schedules were *killing* me.

BUD: Your Yankee stamina got you through.

BETTE: Sure, I'm a tough New Englander. I get that from my mother Ruthie, and my grandmother. I come from a long line of headstrong, and *determined* women. They taught me to be fearless and forthright... a woman has to be, so she can survive in a man's world. Also I'm an Aries, and an Aries is always ready for a fight. I'd become a force to be reckoned with. "What the Hell!" I said to myself. "I'll use that power to benefit *others* working here who deserve better." I felt I owed it to them.

BUD: Bette the Ram! I remember you storming off the set of 'Jezebel', shoulders up and head down, ready to butt the seat of Jack Warner's pants when he threatened to fire William Wyler's ass, for going *way* over the shooting schedule.

BETTE: I'd fight for *anyone* if I thought they were worth it. And Wyler was worth it.

BUD: And what about the time you had to shake the hell out of Miriam Hopkins in 'Old Acquaintance'. That was no act… it was for real.

BETTE: Miriam deserved it! Her behaviour was unprofessional throughout the making of that picture.

BUD: [*Chuckling.*] I recall the entire crew being on set that day to catch you dishing out her punishment.

[BETTE *exits stage left and* BUD *exits stage right as the lights go down to stage black.*]

Scene Nine

1943. A plush apartment film set during the making of 'Old Acquaintance'. Actress MIRIAM HOPKINS and film director VINCENT SHERMAN are in mid-conversation. MIRIAM is slender. She is wearing a full-length evening dress with long sleeves. Her hair is worn up. VINCENT is short, thick-set in build and dark-haired. He is wearing smart-casual clothes.

MIRIAM: … but Vincent darling… if I've asked you once, I've asked you a hundred times to alter the scene. Why does it have to be so *aggressive?*

VINCENT: Because Miriam, dear, and we've gone over this a hundred times, we are going to shoot the scene *exactly* as written. Millie has had it coming to her for a long time and she has to take her punishment. We need to shoot it that way for maximum effect. She's a nasty, jealous bitch and there's no other way of humbling her.

MIRIAM: But to be shaken about in such a heavy-handed fashion? Why, it's positively dangerous. What if she breaks my neck? What then?

VINCENT: [*Aside to the audience.*] Well if she doesn't *I* just might.

MIRIAM: I heard that Vincent! All along, you've taken Bette's side.

VINCENT: [*Angrily.*] I've taken nobody's side. I've been stuck *between* the two of you trying to keep you from scratching each other to pieces. You're worse than a couple of alley cats. [*More subdued.*] Now, please, Miriam. Why can't you be grown up about this? If neither of you mess this up, we should get it in one take. And stop being so precious. Imagine you're a rag doll. It's only acting after all. *That's* what you're being paid to do.

MIRIAM: Well… if *that's* your attitude Vincent, on your own head be it! If I suffer any physical injury, I shall sue you *and* the studio. Now, you can tell that… that… *Jezebel* that I am ready.

[VINCENT *exits stage right, leaving* MIRIAM *pacing the stage and wringing her hands melodramatically.*]

MIRIAM: Oh the sheer humiliation of it is all *too* much.

Optional: [MIRIAM *picks up an empty vase and angrily hurls it at the wall. It shatters into pieces.*] Optional: concludes.

[BETTE DAVIS *age 35, and* VINCENT *enter together stage right. A* CLAPPER BOY *enters stage left.* BETTE *and* MIRIAM a*cknowledge one another by exchanging bitter smiles.*]

VINCENT: Miss Davis, Miss Hopkins! I know you're both going to give me your professional best. [*Aside to* BETTE.] Oh, and Bette… *don't* go easy on her. [*Pauses.*] Everyone, quiet on set! We're going for a take.

CLAPPER BOY: 'Old Acquaintance' scene 102, take 1. [*Claps board.*]

VINCENT: Action!

[KIT (BETTE) *moves toward* MILLIE (MIRIAM) *as if to reprimand her.*]

MIRIAM: Cut! Now Vincent darling, she's not really going to come at me *that* way is she? Like a… like a…

VINCENT: For Heaven's sake Miriam! *I'm* the one who says when we cut. You didn't even give Bette the chance to get out her first line.

BETTE: Come at you like *what* Miriam? You may as well say it since you've begun. I'd welcome a few tips on how *not* to act a scene.

MIRIAM: Now Bette, don't be catty. It's just that you marched over to me like a dock-side worker about to haul a crate. Kit just wouldn't be that burly.

BETTE: Burly! You think *that* was burly? I'll show you what burly really is, if you like.

VINCENT: [*Interjecting before* MIRIAM *can respond.*] Bette it was fine, with just the right amount of directness. And it's just how I want you to do it.

MIRIAM: Well Vincent, if you think you know best…

VINCENT: I *do* know best Miriam, and we are going to go straight for another take. Bette, we'll take it from, "And don't think I couldn't have many times." Now return to your marks. Are we ready? *Yes?* Good!

CLAPPER BOY: 'Old Acquaintance' scene 102, take 2. [*Claps board.*]

VINCENT: And *action!*

BETTE as KIT: And don't think I couldn't have many times. [*Starts to exit.*]

MIRIAM as MILLIE: Alright, go ahead and leave me alone, *all* of you, but you can't take my work away from me. *That* at least is inviolate.

[KIT (BETTE) *in mid exit, stops, and turns to face* MILLIE (MIRIAM).]

MILLIE: (MIRIAM) Well… get out why don't you?

VINCENT: *Cut!* Miriam, the line is "Well… why don't you go? Not, "Well… get out why don't you?"

MIRIAM: [*Exaggerated.*] Dear *me* Vincent, was *that* what I said?

VINCENT: You know *damn well* it was. Now please stick to the script.

MIRIAM: No need to get snippy over a minor slip-up Vincent, darling.

BETTE: Slip-up, my… eye.

VINCENT: *Alright* ladies, let's try again. This time we'll go straight from your line, Miriam.

MIRIAM: Which line is that, Vincent?

VINCENT: You *know* which line, damn it!

[MIRIAM *smiles to herself mischievously.*]

VINCENT: Are we rolling on camera? Right, let's go for a take.

CLAPPER BOY: 'Old Acquaintance' scene 102, take 3. [*Claps board.*]

VINCENT: *Action!*

MILLIE: (MIRIAM) "Well… why don't you…" Arrgh!

[MIRIAM *clasps her hand to her neck and staggers towards the couch. She whimpers, as though in considerable pain.*]

MIRIAM: Oh my neck! My neck! I turned my head rather too fast and something went click. I think I've slipped a vertebra. Oh, the *agony.* Get me a doctor, *somebody,* quickly. I need urgent attention.

BETTE: You have the *urgent attention* of everyone on the set, Miriam. [*To* Vincent.] Let *me* at her Vincent. I'll wring her neck and put us *all* out of our miseries.

MIRIAM: I can do quite well without unfeeling comments of *that* kind, Bette.

BETTE: Then how about this one *with* feeling. It's not a doctor you need, Miriam. It's a fucking *shrink!*

MIRIAM: [*The lights slowly fade to stage black over the following dialogue.*] Oh Vincent. Oh… *Vincent!* That's the limit. I shan't finish the scene. Where *is* that doctor? And *someone…* call my masseuse. Oh, I have to lie down. A pillow… somebody fetch me a pillow.

[*A brief pause. The lights slowly come back up on the same scene. It is an hour later. Tempers are stretched to the limit.* BETTE *has retired to her dressing room.* MIRIAM *and* VINCENT *are seated on the couch. Conversation resumes as the lights begin to go up.*]

VINCENT: Miriam, I'm at the end of my leash. Why won't you openly admit there's really nothing wrong with your neck? Why the melodrama?

MIRIAM: It's a matter of pride. I wouldn't expect you to understand.

VINCENT: I understand *perfectly.* This discord between you and Bette began *not* when you first played together in 'The Old Maid', but before that. It started with 'Jezebel'. It's been festering since *then* and the boil is about to burst. What we have here, plain and simple, is a case of art imitating real life. You are jealous of *Bette's* career in the same way that Millie is jealous of *Kit's.*

MIRIAM: [*Offended.*] Oh! So *you're* the shrink that Bette quite crudely suggested I'm in need of.

VINCENT: No Miriam, but you can't deny this. You played the part of Julie Marsden on stage and the play was a disaster. When *Bette* played Julie in the film, she won her second Academy Award. *That's* what you can't stand.

Your hatred of Bette is such that you are allowing it to ruin what could potentially be your best performance on film. This is not all Bette's picture you know. It's as much yours as it is hers, Miriam. Now, bury the fucking past and do the scene like the experienced pro you are!

[MIRIAM *has been quietly sobbing through* VINCENT*'s rant. He offers her his hand-kerchief. She dries her eyes, blows her nose loudly and responds calmly.*]

MIRIAM: You are *right* Vincent, but my admitting it's true won't change anything. I think me and Bette will always dislike each other, and that's putting it mildly. However, I shall behave myself. Now, let's get on and get it over with, quickly. As you've learned all too well, I'm rarely in a compliant mood.

VINCENT: Will somebody go and tell Bette that Miriam is feeling much better? We're ready to roll.

MIRIAM: I must look a sight.

[A MAKE-UP ASSISTANT *hands* MIRIAM *a mirror.*]

Goodness! I need powder *and* lip rouge.

[*The* MAKE-UP ASSISTANT *powders* MIRIAM*'s face and applies lip rouge, while* BETTE *enters and goes straight to her mark.*]

VINCENT: Now my dears, I sense this take is going to be the one. Miriam, take it from, "Alright, go ahead and leave me," etcetera.

CLAPPER BOY: 'Old Acquaintance' scene 102, take… 13.

VINCENT: *Action!*

MILLIE: (MIRIAM) Alright, *go* ahead and leave me alone, *all* of you. But you can't take my work away from me. *That* at least is inviolate. [KIT (BETTE) *in mid exit, stops, and turns to face* MILLIE (MIRIAM).] Well why don't you go?

KIT: (BETTE) In just a minute.

> [KIT (BETTE) *throws her bag and a parcel onto an armchair as she approaches* MILLIE (MIRIAM). *She takes* MILLIE (MIRIAM) *by her shoulders and shakes her vigorously, about ten times, and then throws her onto the couch.*]

KIT: (BETTE) Sorry!

> [KIT (BETTE) *calmly exits the set and the stage while* MILLIE (MIRIAM) *cries hysterically, pounding her fists on the couch seat.*]

VINCENT: Cut it and print it! There now Miriam, that didn't hurt a bit, did it?

> [*The lights fade to stage black on the set of 'Old Acquaintance'.*]

Scene Ten

1949. A continuation of scene eight.
Lights come up fast. BETTE *and* BUD *have returned to centre stage.*

BETTE: That hussy deserved it! Her habitual tantrums and scene-stealing antics turned around and bit her that day. And Bud, did I enjoy doing it! A 'sherricking' is what my mother Ruthie calls it. As a girl, I was on the receiving end of many a good 'sherricking' from her. She was so damn good at it I couldn't see straight, for days on end. I can barely focus *now*.

BUD: Me neither. This is good whisky.

BETTE: It's the best! I stole it from Jack Warner's office.

BUD: You'd better take it easy now if you wanna get home in one piece. Hand me the bottle. You've kept it company for long enough. Now *sit* down before you fall down!

[BUD *helps* BETTE *to sit and he sits beside her.*]

BETTE: Yes *sir!* But I can hold my liquor as well as any man. I once drank Mr Errol Flynn under the table when he challenged me to a contest, and he's nearly always drunk. That's no *bad* thing. When he's sober, he's intolerable. Bud, the first of my pictures you worked on was 'Elizabeth and Essex', wasn't it? I'm right, am I not?

BUD: You're not wrong Bette!

BETTE: Flynn! A joker if ever there was.

BUD: Sure he was. Remember the scene where he slaps Elizabeth's rear end? We must've had to re-shoot that a dozen times. He slapped so hard your wig came off and with each retake he made you laugh… *out* of character. You were a good sport that day.

BETTE: He did it on purpose of course. He was like a schoolboy, always pulling pranks on me. And he's *not* a good actor… just a pretty face!

I found him immensely attractive, but I didn't submit to his charms. To him, I'd have been another conquest, a new notch on his belt that he could brag about. In our intimate scenes together, I would deliberately stiffen like a damp sheet in a hard frost. Try as he might, he couldn't thaw *me* out. He was notorious on the set for brandishing that *famous* weapon of his and waving it at my ladies-in-waiting. I'm not referring to his prowess as a swordsman either! One of them, bless her, actually fainted when she saw it. Imagine being on the receiving end of *that*.

BUD: Speaking from experience, it wasn't only women he made advances to. He has an eye for the guys as well.

BETTE: Ah ha! So they *aren't* just rumours. Wicked Errol made a play for you did he? My, he's got nerve I'll say that.

BUD: [*Jokingly.*] I didn't respond. Well… he's not my type.

[*They laugh pleasantly and then… silence.*]

BETTE: The studio has been a safe haven and I've been anchored here a long time. Now that it's time to brave the open sea, I'm afraid, Bud! I don't think the public will *ever* take me seriously again after this picture. The critics will feast on it indefinitely. 'Beyond the Forest', could be the final nail in the coffin of Bette Davis. What do *you* think, Bud?

[BUD *is clearly saddened by her honesty and vulnerability but speaks positively.*]

BUD: All the *other* studios will be scrambling over one another to sign you, is what *I* think. No doubt about it! It's a chance they've all been waiting for. That role of a lifetime *is* out there just waiting for you,

Bette, so get up off your sorry ass and *stop wallowing* in the gutter! Now, voyager, sail thou forth to seek and find!

BETTE: Ha! Well said, Bud. Hell, I'm not about to give up as easily as all that. This old dame is still up for a challenge. [*Grumbling.*] Only one thing Bud… my 'sorry ass', as you so *delicately* put it, is numb right down to my ankles! Help me on with my shoes will you? [*She groans through the procedure.*] Now please help me get up. [BETTE *moans and groans from the discomfort as* BUD *hauls her up, then she vigorously rubs her rear.*] There… that's much better. [*Continuing in a mock Southern Belle accent.*] Waah, thaink yah kaand sawr. Ah'm beholden to yah! [*Pauses.*] Seriously Bud, thank you! For turning up when you did, and for lifting me out of the dumps. For all its rewards and the fine friends you make along the way, working in pictures can be a *horribly* lonely existence. I don't feel quite as lonely or afraid now. What time is it?

BUD: A half-past midnight.

BETTE: Hell! It's later than I thought! Little B D will be wondering where the heck her mom's got to. [*With sarcasm.*] My husband might have sent out a search party.

BUD: Another smoke to be goin' with Bette?

BETTE: I better had. I'll send up some smoke signals to let Sherry know I'm on my way home!

[*He lights two simultaneously and offers her one. They draw on their cigarettes deeply, then blow long exhalations of smoke upwards.*]

And how about *you* Bud? Have you someone who's missing you right now?

BUD: [*Suddenly shy and hesitant. Quietly and deeper voiced.*] Oh… well, sure. But, err… he's not exactly gonna be *pacing* the floorboards till I see him. He's gotten used to me working all hours. We've been together a long time…

[BETTE *is taken aback by his admission and her expression is one of amazement.*]

We got hitched in '32 when '42nd Street' went into production. We've been solid ever since. I was an electrician back then and he was a dance coach.

[*The lights go down fast to stage black as* BETTE *and* BUD *exit. The song 'Shuffle Off to Buffalo' plays in the dark while minor changes are made to the existing onstage apartment, which originally served as* MILLIE's *in scene nine.*]

Scene Eleven

September 1932. Apartment interior. Late at night.
Lights up fast. THOMAS, *otherwise known as* THOM, *age 19, is rehearsing his choreographed dance to the tune of 'Shuffle Off to Buffalo' and is using a mop as his dance partner. He dances on and around the furniture, using them as substitute props.* THOM *is athletic, and muscular. He is wearing a white T-shirt, loose pants with turn-ups, white socks and brown Italian loafers. Young* BUD, *age 21, enters the apartment. He is dressed in jeans, a baseball cap worn back-to-front, a bomber-jacket and work boots. The music volume is turned up loud and* THOM, *unaware of* BUD's *presence, continues his dance.* BUD *observes from a distance until* THOM *realises he is not alone.*

BUD: So this is how you spend your nights when I'm working late, huh?

In the company of Ruby Keeler!

THOM: Hey, handsome!

[THOM *puts aside the mop, caresses* BUD*'s cheek and turns off the practice record on the Victrola.*]

How long have you been here?

BUD: [*Indicating the mop with his thumb.*] Long enough to see that I've some pretty stiff competition.

THOM: [*Amusing and brightly dynamic.*] When it comes to Ruby's dancing, 'stiff' is an accurate adjective. *You'd* win the contest hands-down. She dances like she's got a poker stuck up her ass and her timing's lousy. I lost my cool and yelled at her today. "Quit daydreaming Rube! Catch the tempo and get those size nines *off* the floor!" This could be her big break. If she doesn't get the audience's attention right off and keep a hold of 'em through to the end of the number, she's *not* going to win 'em over. She just fixed me with vacant wide eyes like I was joking.

BUD: Well the routine looks good, but can the floor take any more?

[THOM *leaps onto the couch and lounges passively with his hands behind his head.*]

THOM: I hope so. Mrs O'Leary is mad at me. She complained that a piece of the ceiling fell on her head while she was sitting directly below, trying to listen to 'Late Night Theatre' on the radio. She wasn't kidding either. You should've seen her… plaster dust all over, like she was wearing a powdered wig. Threatened to evict me if I don't put it right.

BUD: Maybe you should rent a *ground* floor apartment. Then you can practise all night and not disturb anyone.

THOM: You know, that's not a bad idea... but I told Mrs O I'd get *you* in to fix it Bud.

BUD: Me being the handyman around here?

THOM: Right! On *both* counts.

BUD: Both?

THOM: Well... you're a man, that's for sure and you certainly come in *handy*... if you catch my drift.

[*He stretches his arms out to* BUD. BUD *responds, sits and holds* THOM *in a hard and passionate embrace.*]

BUD: I have my uses.

THOM: Mm, now *that's* a fact...

[*He kisses* BUD *lightly on the nose, quickly releases himself from* BUDs' *arms and gets up off the couch.*]

... and here's another. Mrs O really does want me out, and not just because of the noise *I* make. It's *us!* [*Mimicking* MRS O'LEARY *with her Irish accent.*] ... and while we're about it, I've been thinkin' to me-self that it's *unseemly*, the amount of late-night visits a certain *other* young man is in the habit of makin' to the house. It doesn't look right.

[MRS O'LEARY *has entered the scene and she takes up her*

complaint, speaking directly to the audience. THOM *performs a comical mime to* BUD, *in time, and in keeping with* MRS O's *outburst.* BUD *remains seated.*]

MRS O'LEARY: I'm a respectable woman and I keep a respectable house. I expect my tenants to be decent folks and *not* openly flaunt their… *proclivities…* in such an indiscreet fashion. If one o' *my* sons took to actin' the same way as you, I'd give him such a wallopin' he'd be beggin' the forgiveness of our Holy Virgin Mother and see fit to change his ways, so he would! It's lucky for you that my husband - may the Saints bless him - is dead! He'd have knocked you both into the next world, which in your case would be eternal damnation in the fires of Hell! Now… is that what you two want? Eternal damnation? You're seemingly nice, down-to-earth Catholic boys. Okay, so you're not Irish, but we hold the same beliefs. Come to your senses before it's too late. Find a couple o' nice Catholic girls to settle down with and stop your shenanigans.

THOM: [*To* BUD.] I tried to defend our good names but…

MRS O: [*To the audience, as* THOM *continues to mime.*] … and don't you be tryin' to deny it. Jesus, Mary and Joseph! I live right below you and can hear *everythin'* you and your 'handyman' friend say… and *do*.

[MRS O *recedes into the background and exits.* THOM *resumes impersonating her.*]

THOM: [*As* MRS O.] Handyman? More like *fancy*-man! It'd be better all-round if you were to go. Find *another* house where you can dance… and sin! I shan't be requiring notice.

[BUD *is rolling with laughter on the couch.* THOM *leaps on him and they roll off the sofa onto the rug, laughing themselves out. They kiss hard then* THOM *gets to his feet.*]

THOM: You hungry?

BUD: [*Lazily.*] Starving, though the appetizers weren't bad.

THOM: [*Suggestively.*] No? Well, wait until you try the entrée.

BUD: Oh yeah?

THOM: Yeah! It's in the kitchen. I made your favourite dish. Spaghetti with meatballs! The way to a man's heart and all that…

BUD: [*Sitting upright.*] Open a couple of beers and quit being schmaltzy. You've already got my heart… for as long as you want it.

[BUD *stands and approaches* THOM *with swagger.*]

Why don't we just skip the entrée and go straight to desert?

THOM: Now who's being schmaltzy?

[THOM *removes* BUD's *baseball cap and throws it aside. He is shocked to see that* BUD's *forehead has a deep cut, covered with dried blood.*]

Jesus *Christ* almighty! What the fuck happened, Bud?

BUD: Had another brush with those creeps the next block down. One of 'em came at me with a knife… so I kicked his lousy teeth down his *fuckin'* throat! The cut *ain't* as bad as it looks.

THOM: Come here, baby.

[*He pulls* BUD *towards him by the shoulders and speaks soothingly, with controlled emotion as he licks* BUD*'s wound clean.*]

Those… [*Licks.*] fucking… *wop*… [*Licks.*] bastards.

BUD: [*With irony.*] They say it takes one to know one. [*Pause.*] Let's not kid ourselves Thom. It doesn't matter what part of town we live in or where in the world we go - if they catch on - punks, like those, are gonna be harassing us. [*A pause: then, with joyous exhilaration.*] *Big fucking deal! You're* in my life: that's all that counts and it makes me feel *stronger* than ever I did before… like I could take on the whole *fucking* world. I'm so happy, I could *explode*. I've waited a long time for this. You… the two of us… And I'm not gonna let *anyone* try and stop us. *And* I don't believe Christ *would* damn us for what *we know* is right. It *is* love after all. And I don't *give a fuck* what others might call it.

[THOM *has never felt surer or prouder of* BUD*, than he does now. His love for* BUD *visibly shines out of his face.*]

[BUD*, erupting with anger.*] It's that interfering bitch downstairs with her sanctimonious speeches who should burn in hell. We've put up with *her* brand of bigoted religious crap since we were kids. If it ain't the church or the cops, it's the rest of 'em… like those guys tonight. Getting their kicks from beating up and killing fags. Well, to hell with the lot of 'em! [*Calmer.*] Now we're together, Thom, I'm not afraid any more. I don't feel afraid… of anything. [*Pause.*] Don't y' think it's time that we… we…

THOM: … found a ground floor apartment for the two of us in - the *dis*-reputable queer Utopia that is – down-town Hollywood?

BUD: [*Amused.*] I sprung it too fast. You need time to think about it, maybe?

THOM: I don't need to consider it. I just didn't have the courage to be the first to ask. [*A substantial pause.*] I wanna tell you about a bust-up at the studio canteen today which stopped everyone in their tracks. There was this feisty young actress and she was giving her director as good as *he* was giving out. Apparently he didn't want her cast in his picture, but some other big-shot had overruled him, so he was taking it out on her. Some of those directors can be pretty tyrannical and Michael Curtiz is one of them. He's *not* a guy you talk back to. Watching her stand up to the big man and yell at him, I thought, 'She knows *exactly* what she wants *and* where she's going.' And you know Bud... she's gonna make it. Honestly, her self-confidence was inspiring. [*Short pause.*] She made me realise, right there and then, how much *I'd* be prepared to fight for what I want most in *my* life.

BUD: She sounds formidable.

THOM: She is.

BUD: So... what *is* it you want most?

THOM: [*Lightly teasing* BUD.] To become *the number one* choreographer at Warners, I guess.

BUD: Nothing else?

THOM: Hmm... the money... the glamour... the guys.

BUD: [*Smirking.*] Quit kidding, you joker, and get your butt over here.

[THOM *saunters over to* BUD.]

And what else?

[*They stand face-to-face.* BUD *places his hands on* THOM'*s shoulders.*]

THOM: More than *anything* Bud? You.

[*They kiss passionately.* THOM *takes* BUD'*s hand.*]

Now, come out here… [*He leads* BUD *to the roof garden situated on the rear raised stage. The garden is bathed in a dream-like, misty green light.*] … and dance with me under the stars, in full view of our *respectable* neighbours.

[*Out on the roof garden* BUD *sings 'It Must Be Right, It Can't Be Wrong', as he and* THOM *slow dance to a piano accompaniment.* THOM *sings the first part of the reprise and* BUD *joins* THOM *in the last part of the reprise. As the tune ends,* BUD *and* THOM *kiss softly.*]

Optional: [*A glamorous* TORCH SINGER *enters. She is wearing a full-length, close fitting dress, elbow length gloves and is sparkling with jewelled earrings, bracelets and brooches. Standing forward centre stage, she sings, 'It Must Be Right, It Can't Be Wrong', to a piano accompaniment, while out on the roof garden* BUD *and* THOM, *slow dance to the tune. As the song ends she exits.*]
Optional: concludes.

THOM: [*Quiet intensity.*] Ramon, my love.

BUD: Ti amo, Thomas.

54

[*They kiss again and with arms around each others waists they exit as one, while the misty green light fades to darkness.*
Simultaneously, the lights come up on BETTE *and* BUD *who have returned to front centre stage.*]

Scene Twelve

1949. A continuation of scene ten.

BETTE *and* BUD's *conversation resumes.* BETTE *has taken a gulp of whisky too quickly.*

BETTE: [*Choking.*] Ah! You... have a... a *beau.* I'm... I'm truly astonished. What an unexpected revelation!

[*Aside to the audience.*] And just when I was about to proposition him!

BUD: But you're not shocked?

BETTE: Shocked? No! I'm very broad minded for a New Englander. And, I'm *not* naive about this kind of thing either. Some of my best friends and quite a large number of my fans are, as you might say, 'in the navy'. But I'd never have guessed that about you Bud, not in a million. You're so... you seem so...

BUD: Manly? Normal? Not *all* of us are light on our feet [*Mincing.*] and walk like we've got a dime gripped firmly between the cheeks of our asses, you know.

BETTE: [*Amused by* BUD's *impersonation of an effeminate type.*] No Bud! No! Of course... forgive me Bud. It came as a complete surprise, that's all. Now I really *do* need a drink. Open that other bottle, will you? I'll soon snap out of it.

[BUD *pours a large one into* BETTE's *glass. She takes a big gulp.* BUD *smiles and shakes his head at the irony of the situation.*]

BUD: Where greater men have tried and failed, Buddy Gabrielli actually got Bette Davis to shut the fuck up! [*Pause.*] Y' know Bette, in all the years I've worked here, you're the first person I've told. Now I have, I feel naked. It's nobody else's business anyhow, but it's always been easier *and* safer to keep quiet about it.

BETTE: I admire your courage Bud. There are some things in life that you *must* keep to yourself, until you find a friend you can trust. [*She gently takes* BUD's *hand and continues with quiet sincerity.*] I'm happy that you confided in me, Bud. You *can* trust me to be discreet. Cross my heart. Now, since you managed to stun me into silence, you talk and I'll listen for a change. Go ahead. We don't want this evening to be… all about *me* now do we?

Optional: [*Young* BUD *and young* THOM *enter on the rear raised stage roof garden and enact* BUD's *following monologue in mime. They are enveloped in a green, dream-like misty light.*]

BUD: We first met here, in the canteen. I was eating alone. It was late. There were just a few diners left, some big-league actors who were shooting night scenes. Jimmy Cagney, Ann Dvorak, Edward G. I noticed this handsome young guy on the far side of the room. He was eating alone and was watching me too. The two of us taking furtive glances at first. Then, our eyes locked. The attraction was immediate and I froze, mouth open… loaded fork half way in. [*Pause.*] Bette, did you see 'Spellbound'?

BETTE: The Hitchcock picture?

BUD: Uh-huh.

BETTE: Mm, I loved it.

BUD: Remember the scene where Bergman first claps her eyes on Greg Peck and she's speechless?

BETTE: Course I do. It was love at first sight. What woman wouldn't fall for Gregory Peck at first sight?

BUD: Or what *man?* Well, it was the same as that. My heart was hammering so fast I couldn't breathe. He was grinning at me. I must've looked a complete jerk. His gave me this knowing smile and I knew that *he* knew what I was thinking. He got up, casually walked over, and introduced himself. Real cool-like. Said he was an assistant choreographer but with his incredible good looks, he could've been a romantic leading man. We smoked and talked a while. Turned out he was a new employee with no firm friends, so we arranged to meet up for beers and some bowling. [*Brief pause.*] Who were we tryin' to kid? We knew what we really wanted and became… *physical* you might say, right away. [*Brief pause.*] Being a dancer, boy… was he in good shape.

Optional: [*At this point, young* BUD *and young* THOM *are kissing passionately. The misty green light fades as the dream-like mime ends and they exit the rear stage together.*] Optional: concludes.

BETTE: This *Adonis* of yours has a name I take it?

BUD: Thomas, but he prefers Thom.

BETTE: Thom… I like that. A good, strong name.

BUD: My personal life was lonely until Thom came along. I'd hang out with guys from the film crew after work. Unwind over beers and cards. Eye the dames along with 'em. Joke about queers. Acting like a regular Joe, *hoping* that one of the guys was made like me. Wondering if I'd ever make that connection, 'n' quit havin' to act.

BETTE: But how could you stand it, Bud?

BUD: [*Shrugging.*] A solitary life's not so bad once you get used to it. Oh, I could've cruised for pick-ups in the Hollywood hills, or in steam rooms and back-street dives. Paid for a fuck with some low-life even! But that's not my style and *way* too risky. I didn't wanna blow my cover *or* my job, so I continued to play it straight and wait until another play-acting Joe like me showed up. Someone steady, and courageous enough to try at somethin' like commitment. You might say it was love I was after.

BETTE: And you found your regular guy in Thom?

BUD: [*Almost purring.*] Yeah… and it was *some* fire we started back then. [*He takes a long gulp from the whisky bottle and sets it down between him and* BETTE.] It's still smouldering away. Every now and then we throw another log on the fire, and when we do… oh *boy…* you can feel the heat all over Hollywood!

BETTE: Is it me, or has the night suddenly turned sultry? [*They laugh pleasantly, then* BETTE *becomes serious.*] Where *my* relationships with men are concerned, I *invite* disaster. My two previous marriages ended badly and this one with Sherry is going nowhere fast. I hold with the old-fashioned notion of love, marriage, fidelity… the whole package. But before long, I get bored playing housewife and start to break it up. My failing is I will *never* submit to a man. Could *any* man, be content, living in the shadow of Bette Davis? I doubt it. [*Holding up her glass of whisky.*] Too much of *this* when I'm around Sherry brings out my mean streak… before long the fists start to fly. I'm ashamed to admit it, but my darling little girl has witnessed *that*. [*She pauses and shudders with regret.*] I behave like a spoiled young *brat* who can't control her temper. I *must* get my own way Bud, regardless of whether I'm right or wrong. I've become one *bitch* of a bully and *no-one* loves a bully. The result is I'm disliked, hated even. Not many people know this but I've even had attempts made on my life. *Here…* at the studio. Oh, I've made some enemies along the way but *I* am my own worst enemy. I live by *my* rules, but by doing so, I've consigned myself to a life of loneliness. Loneliness… that's the price I pay. [*Pause.*] There! Now *I*, being the life and soul of the party, have well and truly cheered you up! [*Pause.* BUD *looks at her sympathetically.*] Life is a lonely thing Bud, unless one meets the right person to share it with. I *know* Sherry isn't the one for me. I still haven't found the right person and I'm not sure that I ever will. But *you* have! Cherish him, Bud. Keep those embers glowing and you'll never be lonely again. Now… I *insist* that I give you a goodbye hug!

[*They hug briefly and gently.* BETTE *gives* BUD *an affectionate kiss on the cheek.*]

Optional: [*The lights fade as they step apart and* BETTE *moves to front centre stage. She remains standing, and lit by a medium spot she sings 'Life is a Lonely Thing', to a piano accompaniment. The lights come up slowly at the conclusion of the song.*] Optional: concludes.]

[BETTE *collects her purse and places her Academy Award statuette inside it.*]

BUD: Bye Bette and don't be a stranger now, y' hear? [*Suddenly animated.*] Bette, wait! Y' gotta make a grand exit. Leave in *style*. It's your final scene and for once, I get to direct it! You're Rosa Moline and you're desperate to break out of this dead-end town. There's gotta be somethin' *better* out there. The windy city's callin' to you! Chicago, Chicago, Chicago… Now, *action!*

BETTE: [*As* ROSA MOLINE. *Magnificently over-acting.*] *What* a *dump!* If I don't get out of here, I'll die! If I don't get out of here, I *hope* I die! [*Howling with raucous laughter.*] If I don't get out of here I'll end up in the booby-hatch!

[BUD *joins in the laughter. Their joviality subsides.* BUD *takes his cigarette pack out of his shirt pocket. It is empty.*]

BUD: I'd offer you one for the road but I'm all out. [*He screws up the pack and tosses it.*]

BETTE: Then why not have one of mine?

BUD: [*Mouth agape.*] You *devil* for holding out on me!

BETTE: [*Taking a gold cigarette case from her purse.*] Well, you ought to have *guessed* that Bette Davis *never* runs out of cigarettes. I always keep some in reserve in case an emergency situation arises. Here… take one! [*She hands him the cigarette case.*]

BUD: It's inscribed.

BETTE: You may read it.

BUD: Is it personal?

BETTE: Very, but not necessarily private.

BUD: [*Reads aloud.*] "An actor is something less than a man; an actress is *more* than a woman."

BETTE: Every time I smoke a cigarette, it serves as a constant reminder of the sexual inequality of women in this male dominated industry.

[BUD *lights two cigarettes and hands one to* BETTE, *along with the cigarette case. Simultaneously, they inhale deeply and exhale slowly.*]

It's the essence of what Mother instilled in me all those years ago when I first arrived in Hollywood, and it's given me courage when I've *badly* needed it.

BUD: I'd wish you luck Bette, but you don't need it. Formidable lady, I'll walk you to your car.

[BETTE *is still a little unsteady on her feet.*]

You're in *no* fit state to drive.

BETTE: No? I've practically *talked* myself sober.

BUD: No! Tonight I'm your chauffeur. I'll drive you home. [*Playfully.*] Your carriage awaits… Queen Elizabeth. Now! Hand over the keys!

BETTE: No Bud! You're a true gentleman and I thank you for your kindness, but no. I'm Ruth Elizabeth Davis! I make my own decisions, always have, and I'm *not* about to rely on any man. Even one as well-intentioned as yourself. I may have exceeded my limit, so there might be a bumpy ride ahead… but I'm ready for it. Now, I'm out of here! [*She begins to sing raucously.*]

"I'll go home and get my panties,
you go home and get your scanties…"

[BUD *joins in as* BETTE *links her arm in his.*]

BETTE & BUD: "… and away we'll go. Ooh-ooh-ooh.
Off we're gonna shuffle, shuffle off to Buffalo."

[*During the second verse they shimmy off the stage and make an aisle exit.*]

"To Niag'ra in a sleeper,
there's no honeymoon that's cheaper,
and the train goes slow. Mmm-mmm-mmm.
Off we're gonna shuffle, shuffle off to Buffalo".

[*As their song ends, the introductory title music of the film 'All About Eve' fades in and plays to its conclusion while the whole cast return to the stage and take their bows.*]

THE END

Act One

The Alley Duse

Alternative Scene One

Saturday 13th December 1930. Midday.
Railway Station Platform. Pasadena, California USA.
Stage actress BETTE DAVIS, age 22, and her mother RUTHIE have
arrived by train and are waiting for an escort to take them to the
UNIVERSAL FILM STUDIO. Both are smartly but plainly dressed.
BETTE has BOO, her young wire haired fox terrier tucked under one
arm. BETTE is tired and irritable from the long, cross-country journey
and she is pacing the platform agitatedly. It is a hot, bright sunny day.

BETTE: God damn it, Mother! There's nobody here. They've forgotten us.

RUTHIE: Don't curse Bette dear, and don't worry so. You *know* I wired
Mr Johnston before we boarded the train in Chicago. He's expecting
us.

BETTE: Then *where's* the escort he promised?

RUTHIE: Someone is bound to turn up eventually. Why don't you take
Boo and go sit in the waiting room? I'll stay here.

BETTE: [*Rubbing her rear.*] We've been sitting for more than *five days* on
that blasted train Mother, travelling at a snails pace through countless
miles of snowdrifts with frozen asses. *I* don't mean to sit down again
for a week.

RUTHIE: Please Bette, 'backsides' or 'rear ends' are quite adequate and acceptable alternatives, you know.

[*They laugh pleasantly.*]

We should thank our lucky stars we are in sunny California. [*She breathes in deeply and exhales loudly.*] What a lovely day! Saturday December 13, 1930 is one we should always remember my love. The start of your career in motion pictures!

BETTE: Isn't it strange? Only twelve days to Christmas and it's like the middle of a New England July.

[*They stand soaking up the sun appreciatively.* MR HARPER, *a representative of UNIVERSAL PICTURES makes his entrance via the aisle but stands a way apart from* BETTE *and* RUTHIE, *scrutinising them. He is of medium height with a thin moustache and hair slicked flat, wearing a plain suit and carrying his hat. He is slightly effeminate and fussy – reminiscent of a combination of Eric Blore and Franklin Pangborn.*]

BETTE: Look Mother! That odd little man over there. Do you suppose…

[BOO *barks repeatedly as* MR H *approaches* BETTE *and* RUTHIE. MR H *dabs at his perspiring forehead with a handkerchief. He stands between the two women, addressing* BETTE, *oblivious to* RUTHIE.]

MR H: Pardon me, but are you by chance a Miss Davis?

BETTE: I am.

MR H: Miss Bette Davis?

64

BETTE: That's right.

MR H: I'm Mr Percival Harper. [*He takes* BETTE's *free hand and shakes it vigorously.*] On behalf of Mr Carl Laemmle and Mr Laemmle Jr. of Universal Pictures, I'd like to welcome you my dear. I hope your journey was a pleasant one?

BETTE: Barely tolerable, but as you see, I survived it.

[*Still holding her hand,* MR H *looks* BETTE *up and down from head to toe.*]

MR H: Well… my dear… you're not what I was expecting. No, not at all. I'd imagined you to be quite… different.
[BETTE, *taken aback, rapidly withdraws her hand.*]

BETTE: *How* different, *Mr* Harper?

MR H: You don't look like any actress *I've* met, my dear. Not one bit.

BETTE: [*Sharply, due to his directness.*] Is that so? Just what kind of person *did* you expect? A pouting, peroxide blonde perhaps?

MR H: You jest my dear, but at the very *least,* you should own a fur coat and wear *expensive* perfume. The very best. Mitsouko! Shalimar! Not… [*He sniffs the air, disapprovingly.*] Lily of the Valley.

BETTE: A fur coat for the journey here *would* have been both welcome and practical, but in this heat. Are you kidding, Mr Harper?

MR H: My dear young lady, I'm serious. From today, your public image is of paramount importance. In a crowd of *ordinary* people, you have to stand out larger than life, and cultivate a personal style all your own to set you apart from your peers. Then there's Mr *Laemmle* to please. *His* priority will be to see how your gams rate.

BETTE: My what?

MR H: Your legs! He appreciates a good shapely leg on a well-dressed woman.

BETTE: That may be, but what have my *legs* got to do with acting?

MR H: [*Droll and bitchy.*] My dear… it's *clear* you're new to Hollywood. [*He circles* BETTE *once, looking her over, speaking at the same time.*] Your little doggy here *does* lend you a vague artistic… *some*-thing, but *you* will have to be completely made over.

[*He attempts to stroke* BOO's *head, but thinks again and withdraws his hand when* BOO *growls and snaps at him.*]

MR H: [*Flustered.*] There… nice doggy. [MR H *dabs nervously at his forehead with his handkerchief.*] Err… where was I?

BETTE: You were expressing how plain I look.

MR H: Now please, my dear, I don't mean to imply *anything* of the kind. Good gracious no. But, you have to admit, you're no bird of paradise, more like a little brown wren *I'd* say. Never mind, we'll take care of *that*. Now, if you will allow me, I have a car waiting to take you to the Hollywood Plaza Hotel and, from there, to meet Mr Laemmle.

[*He turns, dismounts the stairs and waits halfway down the aisle.* BETTE *and* RUTHIE *laugh in disbelief at his complete lack of subtlety.*]

BETTE: [*To* RUTHIE] Welcome to California! Hold my arm, Mother. I feel the insuperable urge to slap that man. Will *all* studio executives be so damned rude I wonder?

RUTHIE: I think our Mr Harper is more likely to be a mere lackey. Mr Laemmle's pumped up errand boy.

BETTE: [*Calls out.*] Oh, Mr Harper!

[MR H *returns to centre stage.*]

You *may* not have noticed this lady patiently waiting. It is my mother. She is going to accompany me when I meet with Mr Laemmle.

[MR H *nervously acknowledges* RUTHIE.]

MR H: I beg your pardon my dear lady. [*He takes* RUTHIE's *hand and bends to kiss it but thinks twice and drops it, due to her angry expression.*] Pleased to… er… make your acquaintance I'm sure. [*To* BETTE.] Dear Miss Davis… or might I call you Bette?

BETTE: Bette… *if* you must.

MR H: Mr Laemmle will *insist* on seeing you alone Bette. He doesn't approve of stage mothers tagging along.

RUTHIE: *Really?* Well I'm hardly one of *those* Mr Harper. You should get to know me a little better before making an assumption of *that* kind.

MR H: I can tell you now, it's extremely unlikely that a mother of *any* kind will get her foot in the door of Mr Laemmle's office.

BETTE: Then, Mr Harper, this will be one of those rare occasions where one *does*. Where I go, Mother goes, or I don't go at all. Why, she's given up almost everything she owns to finance this trip and if it weren't for her complete faith in my talent, I'd not be here today. [*She slips an arm around* RUTHIE*'s waist. Looking directly at* RUTHIE, *she speaks with sincere affection.*] Ruthie, you are nothing short of being a saint! [*Turning her head to address* MR H.] And when I'm a star, I'll see she lives in a style that befits a star's mother.

MR H: My oh my, you're an outspoken young lady aren't you my dear? Film Star indeed! You *are* in a hurry. Well nobody could say you're not determined. [*To* RUTHIE, *still very flustered.*] Ruth… er… *Mrs* Davis. I hope that you can persuade Bette to hold her fire when she meets Mr Laemmle. Her future at Universal might depend on it.

RUTHIE: I am responsible for nurturing Bette's independent spirit, Mr Harper. She doesn't require my advice when it comes to dealing with studio heads or making her own career decisions. Do you, love?

BETTE: Certainly not!

RUTHIE: Even if she *does* hang herself in the process. [*Brief pause.*] But a word of warning. If you ever light Bette's fuse, stand as far away as possible as quickly as you can. It's a very short one.

MR H: [*Ruffled and resigned.*] Very well madam, after this little demonstration I think I shall take that as good advice. We had better be getting along.

[MR H *leaves the stage via the stairs and begins a slow exit via the aisle.*]

BETTE: Don't be fooled, Mother. I'm nervous *and* apprehensive on the inside.

RUTHIE: Our Mr Harper doesn't know that, does he? You fooled *him*. Be tough with these guys Bette. Have 'em by the balls from the word go. It's a man's world my love, so you're going to have to be *more* than a woman if you mean to rise in it. Show them you mean business – they'll take you seriously.

BETTE: If you weren't here, Mother, I'd be on the next train back home.

RUTHIE: I'll stick around for as long as you need me. For the duration if you like.

[MR H *calls to them from the aisle.*]

MR H: Well ladies, have you changed your minds?

[BETTE *and* RUTHIE *exchange amused glances.*]

BETTE: Lead on Mr Harper.

[BETTE *links her arm in* RUTHIE'*s*. BOO *resumes his yapping as they march off stage via the steps and exit, following* MR H *via the aisle.*]

RUTHIE: Let battle commence!

SHUFFLE OFF TO BUFFALO: act one: scene two
Al Dubin / Harry Warren

BETTE DAVIS:
I'll go home and get my panties,
you go home and get your scanties,
and away we'll go. Ooh-ooh-ooh.
Off we're gonna shuffle, shuffle off to Buffalo!

To Niag'ra in a sleeper,
there's no honeymoon that's cheaper.
And the train goes slow. Mmm-Mmm-Mmm.
Off we're gonna shuffle, shuffle off to Buffalo!

For a little silver quarter,
we can have the Pullman porter
turn the lights down low. Ooh-Ooh-Ooh.
Off we're gonna…

[*Now on stage, she ceases singing abruptly. A brief pause.*]

THEY'RE EITHER TOO YOUNG OR TO OLD: act one: scene four
Frank Loesser / Arthur Shwartz

BETTE DAVIS:
They're either too young or too old.
They're either too fast or too fast asleep.
So darling believe me I'm yours to keep.
There isn't any gravy, the gravy's in the navy.

I'VE WRITTEN A LETTER TO DADDY: act one: scene four
Frank De-Vol / Bob Merrill

BETTE DAVIS as BABY JANE HUDSON:
>I've written a letter to Daddy,
>His address is heaven above.
>I've written "Dear Daddy, we miss you
>And wish you were with us to love".
>
>Instead of a stamp, I put kisses.
>The postman says, that's best to do.
>I've written a letter to Daddy
>Saying "I love you".

GROWING OLDER, FEELING YOUNGER: act one: scene four
Norman Newell / Roger Webb

BETTE DAVIS:
>Do you really have to say in your understanding way,
>what I've always known, but never faced the truth?
>There's a world that's for the young,
>a time when golden songs are sung,
>but age can very rarely mix with youth.
>When a girl is over 30, well *40*, if you must!
>To have a mind of 20 seems a little bit unjust.
>
>[Chorus.] Growing older, feeling younger.
>What can we do? Time is so fleeting.
>April fools us, Winter rules us.
>Autumn and Spring, they have no meeting.
>Love comes along, there is the danger.
>Truth is the mirror, youth is a stranger.
>Growing older, feeling younger.
>Why can't time stand still?
>
>[Verse 2.] There's a truth you have to face,
>that you can't keep up the pace of a man who's maybe 20, 25.
>But from time to time, you find
>a man, who has the kind of mind
>that makes you feel it's *good* to be alive.
>Even so, the years pass by and Autumn comes too soon.
>Though your mind may pay the piper, it's your body calls the tune.
>
>[Chorus repeated.]

IT MUST BE RIGHT, IT CAN'T BE WRONG: act two: scene eleven
Kim Gannon / Max Steiner

BUD: Wrong. Would it be wrong to kiss?
Seeing as I feel like this, would it be wrong to try?

Wrong. Would it be wrong to stay… here in your arms this way,
under this starry sky?

If it is wrong, then why were you sent to me?
Why am I content to be with you forever?

So, when I need you so much… and I have waited so long.
It must be right, it can't be wrong.

THOM: If it is wrong, then why were you sent to me?
Why am I content to be with you forever?

BUD and THOM: So, when I need you so much… and I have waited so
long. It must be right, it can't be wrong.

LIFE IS A LONELY THING: act two: scene twelve
George David Weiss / Joe Sherman

BETTE: [*Spoken.*] All things in this world have a reason for being.
     Meaning, direction, aim.
     The whys and wherefores may surely elude *us*;
     the pawns in this heavenly game.
     But the mystical formula goes on.
     Earth spins, day breaks, night falls,
     with reason and rhyme. With reason and rhyme.

     [*Sung.*] What good is a bud that won't blossom?
     A rose that refuses to flower?
     Of what earthly use is an April day
     that hasn't the good sense to shower?

     What purpose a brook that won't murmur?
     A crocus that doesn't mean Spring?
     What good is a phone that just sits there
     and sits there and just won't ring?

     Oh, life is a lonely thing. Oh, life is a lonely thing.

     [*The lights come up slowly at the conclusion of the song.*] Optional:
     concludes.

74

Acknowledgements

My very special thanks to

John R F Richardson for your invaluable contribution to
MORE THAN A WOMAN in the early stages of development.

also

Susannah Greenan

Barbara Penny-Toure

Craig Liney

Andrew Dunn

Stephanie and Paul Carey

and L U Theatre & The Original Cast and Team

for your invaluable contributions and opinions, which gave me
new perspectives on the story and characters as I developed the
play from initial written drafts through to completion.

MORE THAN A WOMAN by Russell Liney

    I confess that although I've enjoyed watching Bette Davis on film, I know very little about her, other than her reputation as a diva. So it was fascinating to watch this play based on key incidents in her career, which challenged that reputation and put it in context.

Starting with her arrival in Hollywood, escorted by her strong and supportive mother, Bette immediately appears as independent, ambitious, and unafraid of voicing her opinions. Universal Pictures are more interested in her looks than her ability, but this is an attitude Bette refuses to bow to. Her early career at Warner Brothers is characterised by frequent spats with studio head Jack Warner. Although he attempts to sideline her by casting her in second-rate films, Bette is not to be deterred, and succeeds in becoming one of the most famous, Oscar-winning actresses of the Golden Age of film. But it's not without pain.

The play is cleverly structured in that an older Bette; drunk and maudlin, confides in lighting engineer Bud Gabrielli and reflects on the path of her career, which is told in a series of flashbacks, highlighted by the struggles she has faced at the studio and the strength she gained from her mother's support, which gave her the self-belief and courage necessary, to succeed as a woman in a man's world. She has indeed had to be "more than a woman".

This is counter-pointed by Bud's own story of his same-sex relationship, and of how he has had to disguise his true self from an intolerant society, the play highlights the flip-side of the Golden Age to show how people adopt different strategies in order to survive and thrive. The story is moving, and still very pertinent: the film industry is still rife with sexism, and homophobia in the workplace and in society is all too prevalent. By holding up a mirror, the struggles of the past reflect the continuing struggles of the present. The play is frequently funny. Miss Murgatroyd, Jack Warner's secretary, cheekily subverts his instructions and his rages. Thom's Irish/ American landlady Mrs O'Leary's tirade against the "boy and his handyman" living upstairs is hilarious, and Miriam Hopkins's 'punishment' literally carried out at the hands of Bette Davis is pure screwball comedy.

The actors portraying all the roles in the play are excellent. Bette's sheer physical presence, ably played by Francesca Leone and Emily Dilworth is spot on, really conveying the feistiness of Bette as both a performer and a person. Bryanie Whittingham-Ball doubling as Miss Murgatroyd and actress Miriam Hopkins almost steals the show. Ben Crome as Jack Warner clearly thoroughly enjoyed being nasty (although bested every time by Bette!) and Alex Hatcher's role as Bud is nicely understated, hitting just the right note as an 'outsider' with a genuine personality working inside an industry steeped in superficiality. Russell's play is finely observed and crafted with great affection for his subject, his passion for this era of film-making shining through. He commented to me after the play's second performance that his aim was to portray strong, three-dimensional women, surviving by their wits in an industry governed and populated by two-dimensional men. I certainly feel that he succeeded: Bette's story is quite inspirational, and it's given me a new perspective on the old films that I've watched (and have yet to discover). Well done Russell on a brilliant début! In the hope of more plays to come.

Jo Westwood: The Tangled Leaves of Anniseed.

Bette Davis as Rosa Moline

In the 1949 film

Beyond The Forest